PERCUSSION 1 & 2

PERFORMANCE FAVORITES

Volume 1

Band Arrangements Correlated with Essential Elements® 2000 Band Method Book 2

ISBN 1-423-45788-9

7777 W. Bluemound Rd. P.O. Box 13819 Milwaukee, WI 53213

00860200

AFRICAN SKETCHES

(Based on African Folk Songs)

PERCUSSION 1
(Shaker (Maracas), Tamb.)

JAMES CURNOW (ASCAP)

AFRICAN SKETCHES

(Based on African Folk Songs)

PERCUSSION 2
(Tri., Sus. Cym., S.D.)

JAMES CURNOW (ASCAP)

BARRIER REEF

Overture For Band

PERCUSSION 1
(Snare Drum, Bass Drum)

JOHN HIGGINS (ASCAP)

BARRIER REEF

Overture For Band

PERCUSSION 2
(Cr. Cym., Tambourine, Triangle, Sus. Cym.)

JOHN HIGGINS (ASCAP)

00860200

DO YOU HEAR WHAT I HEAR

PERCUSSION 1
S.D., B.D.

Words and Music by
NOEL REGNEY and GLORIA SHAYNE
Arranged by MICHAEL SWEENEY

DO YOU HEAR WHAT I HEAR

Words and Music by
NOEL REGNEY and GLORIA SHAYNE
Arranged by MICHAEL SWEENEY

PERCUSSION 2
Finger Cym., Sus. Cym., Sleigh Bells, Tri., Cr. Cym.

00860200

PERCUSSION 1
(Snare Drum, Bass Drum)
JOHN MOSS (ASCAP)
Stately March
S.D.
B.D.
cresc. poco a poco

REGIMENTAL HONOR

PERCUSSION 2
(Sus. Cym., Tri., Cr. Cym.)

JOHN MOSS (ASCAP)

00860200

Recorded by BLOOD, SWEAT, & TEARS

SPINNING WHEEL

Words and Music by
DAVID CLAYTON THOMAS
Arranged by MICHAEL SWEENEY

PERCUSSION 1
(S.D., B.D.)

*Lay left stick across drum head and strike with right stick.

Recorded by BLOOD, SWEAT, & TEARS

SPINNING WHEEL

Words and Music by
DAVID CLAYTON THOMAS
Arranged by MICHAEL SWEENEY

PERCUSSION 2
(Cowbell, Sus. Cym., Tamb.)

0860200

THE STREETS OF MADRID

THE STREETS OF MADRID

PERCUSSION 2
(Tambourine, Sus. Cym., Med. Triangle, Woodblock or Castanets)

JOHN MOSS

YOU'RE A GRAND OLD FLAG

PERCUSSION 1
S.D., B.D.

Words and Music by GEORGE M. COHAN
Arranged by PAUL LAVENDER

YOU'RE A GRAND OLD FLAG

PERCUSSION 2
Triangle, Cr. Cym.

Words and Music by GEORGE M. COHAN
Arranged by PAUL LAVENDER

BRITISH MASTERS SUITE

PERCUSSION 1
Snare Drum, Bass Drum

Arranged by JOHN MOSS

I. Marching Song

GUSTAV HOLST

Moderate Stately March

S.D.
B.D.

f [5] 3 *mp*

mp *mf* 3 *mp* *mf* [13] 3

mp *mf* *mp* *mf* *mp* *f*

mp *mf* [22] (*mf*)

f

[29] *p* *f*

II. Nimrod (From "Enigma Variations")

EDWARD ELGAR

Very slow with emotion

III. Sine Nomine

RALPH VAUGHAN WILLIAMS

BRITISH MASTERS SUITE

PERCUSSION 2
Cr. Cym., Sus. Cym., Tri.

Arranged by JOHN MOSS

I. Marching Song

GUSTAV HOLST

II. Nimrod (From "Enigma Variations")

EDWARD ELGAR

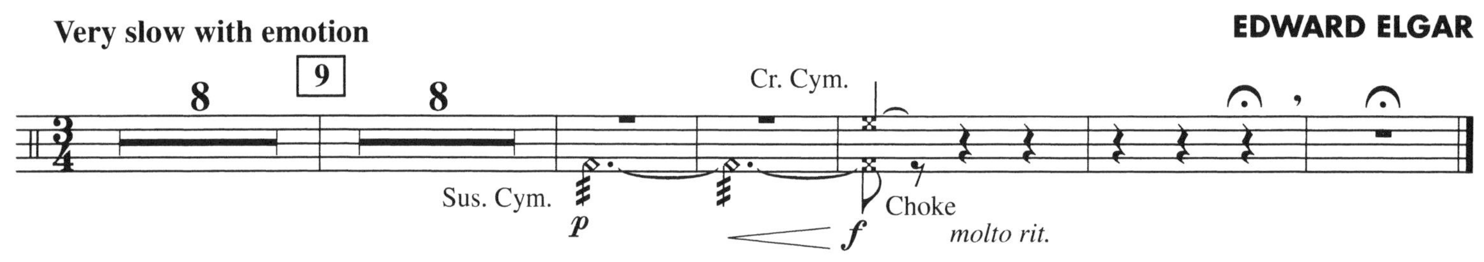

III. Sine Nomine

RALPH VAUGHAN WILLIAMS

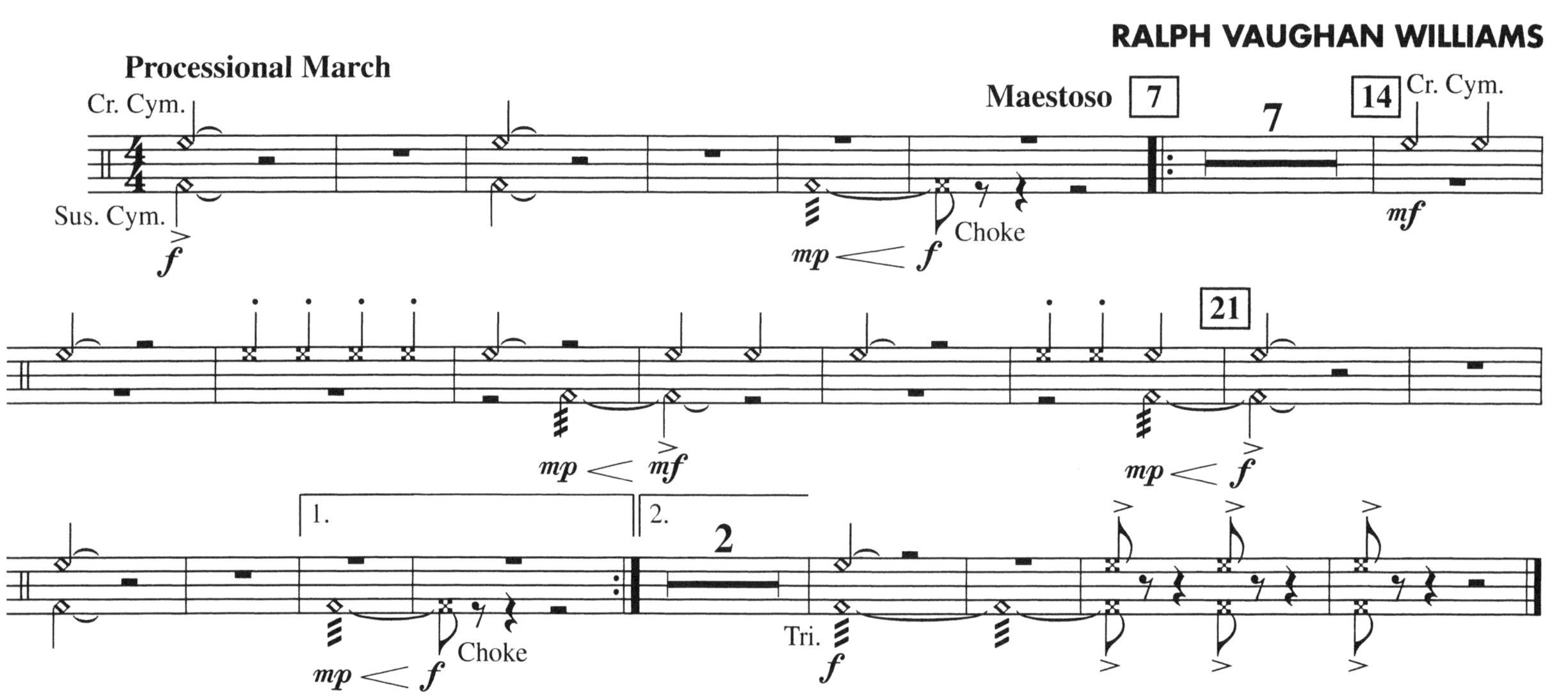

(This page left intentionally blank for a page turn.)

ELVES' DANCE
(From The Nutcracker)

PERCUSSION 1
(Snare Drum, Bass Drum)

PETER I. TCHAIKOVSKY
Arranged by PAUL LAVENDER

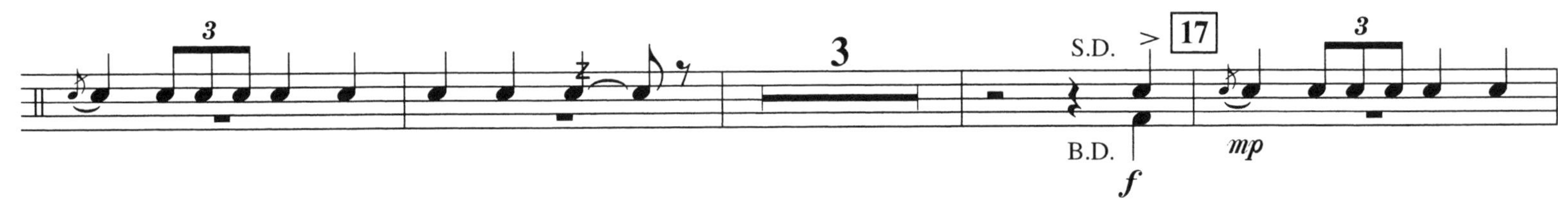

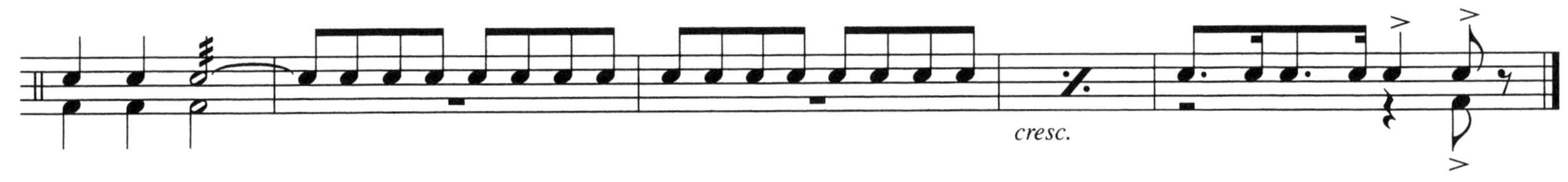

ELVES' DANCE
(From The Nutcracker)

PERCUSSION 2
(Temple Blocks, Triangle, Ratchet, Cr. Cym.)

PETER I. TCHAIKOVSKY
Arranged by PAUL LAVENDER

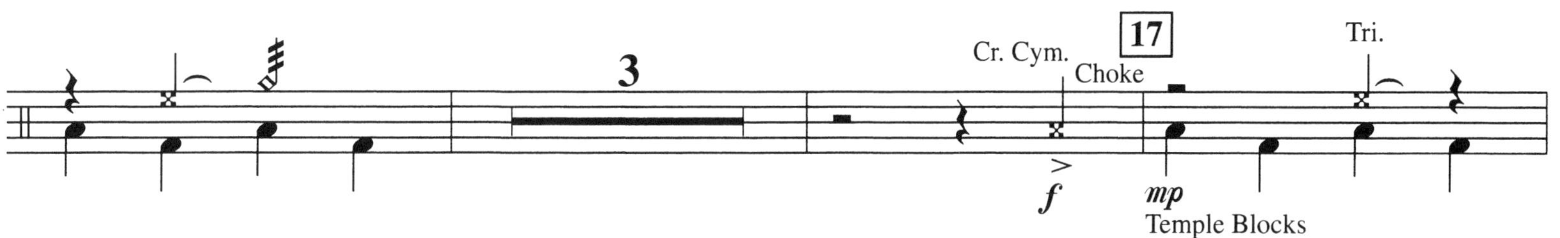

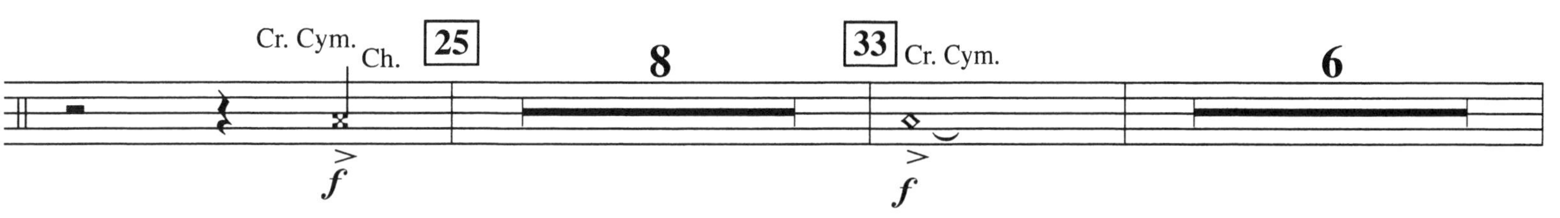

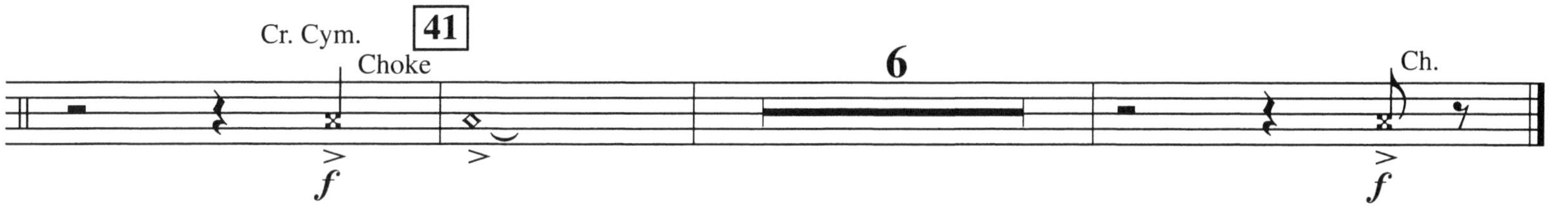

FI EBIRD SUITE Finale

FIREBIRD SUITE – Finale

GAELIC DANCES

PERCUSSION 1
(Snare Drum, Bass Drum)

Arranged by JOHN MOSS

42
f
f
46
8
54
mf
1.
2.
64
fp
f
f
68
76
f
1.
2.
mp
88
f
ff

GAELIC DANCES

PERCUSSION 2
(Sus. Cym., Medium Tri., Wood Block, Tambourine)

Arranged by JOHN MOSS

Sus. Cym.
(with sticks)
mp
mf
1.
2.
mp
mf
64
f
with mallets
68
f
mp
76
mp
Tri.
f
1.
2.
mp
mp
Sus. Cym.
(with mallets)
88
f
mp
ff

IRISH LEGENDS

PERCUSSION 1
Large Tri., S.D.

JAMES CURNOW (ASCAP)

00860200

IRISH LEGENDS

PERCUSSION 2
Sus. Cym., Tamb.

JAMES CURNOW (ASCAP)

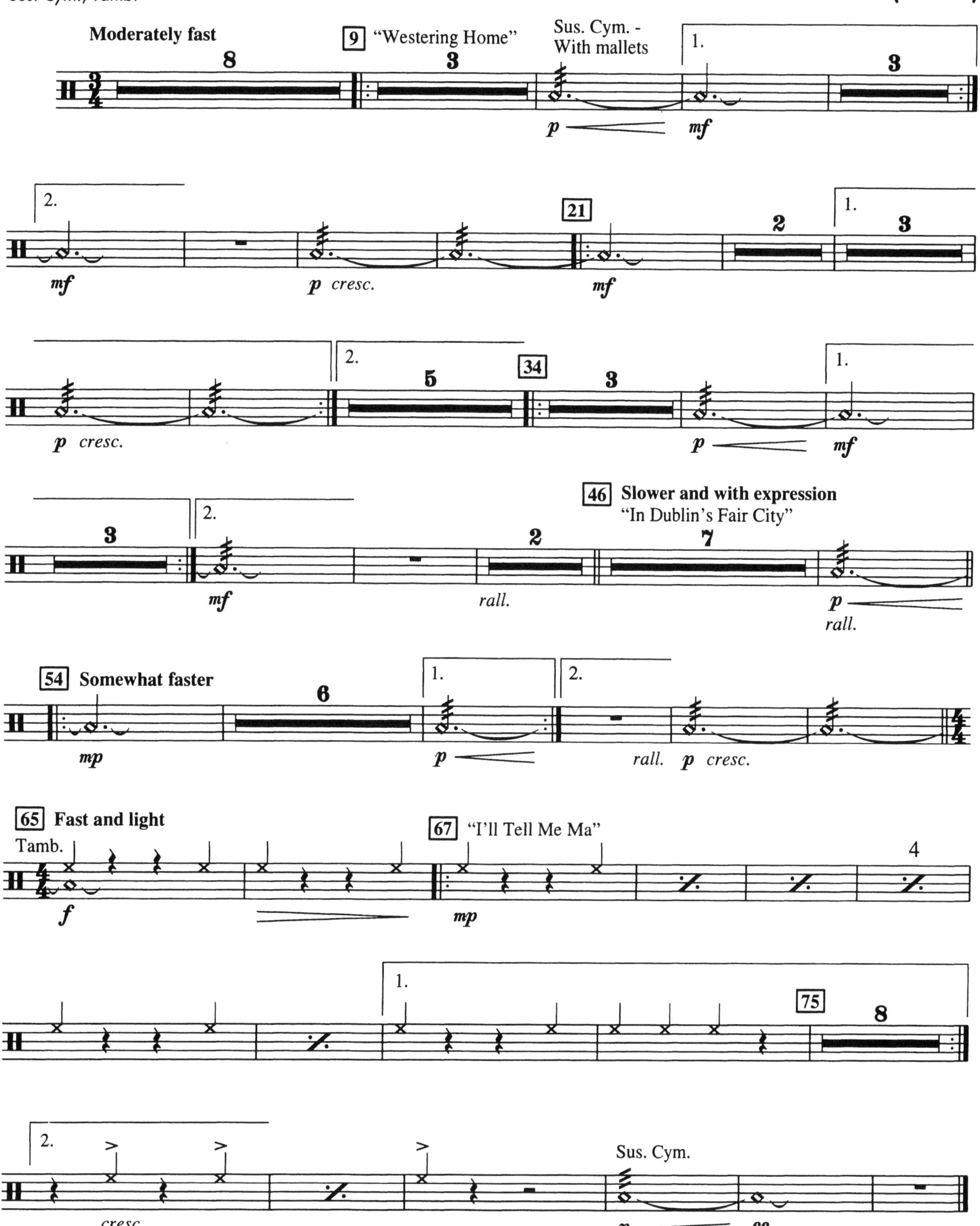

ON BROADWAY

PERCUSSION 1
S.D., B.D., Hi-Hat, Ride Cym.

Words and Music by BARRY MANN, CYNTHIA WEIL, MIKE STOLLER and JERRY LEIBER
Arranged by MICHAEL SWEENEY

Medium Rock Groove

S.D. B.D. *f* Stick on Hi-Hat Rim Knock *mf*

On S.D. Head *fp* *f* 8 *mf* 2 2

16 On Cym. dome Rim Knock

Hi-Hat 2 2 Ride Cym. *mp*

28 *mf*

36 On Cym. dome + Rim Knocks On S.D. Head *f*

Hi-Hat *mf* *mp*

48 2 2

56 Ride Cym. *mf*

f

00860200

ON BROADWAY

PERCUSSION 2
Cowbell, Shaker, Vibraslap

Words and Music by BARRY MANN, CYNTHIA WEIL, MIKE STOLLER and JERRY LEIBER
Arranged by MICHAEL SWEENEY

Written for the 100th Anniversary Celebration of the Modern Olympic Games

SUMMON THE HEROES

(For Tim Morrison)

PERCUSSION 1
S.D., B.D.

By JOHN WILLIAMS
Arranged by MICHAEL SWEENEY

Written for the 100th Anniversary Celebration of the Modern Olympic Games

SUMMON THE HEROES

(For Tim Morrison)

PERCUSSION 2
Tom-Tom, Cr. Cym., Sus. Cym., Tri.

By JOHN WILLIAMS
Arranged by MICHAEL SWEENEY

TWO CELTIC FOLKSONGS

(The Maids of Mourne Shore • The Star of the County Down)

PERCUSSION 1
Low Tom, Bass Drum, Snare Drum

Celtic Folksongs
Arranged by PAUL LAVENDER

Dolce 4

5 "The Maids of Mourne Shore" 6

Slightly Faster 2

13 8

21 4

Tempo I 2

rit.

With Energy
Low Tom
B.D.
f

33 "The Star of the County Down"

4

8

41 2

mp *mf*
S.D.
mf

2

mp *mf*
mf

47

4

Slowly 2

A Tempo
Low Tom
B.D.
f

TWO CELTIC FOLKSONGS

(The Maids of Mourne Shore • The Star of the County Down)

PERCUSSION 2
Sus. Cym., Castanets, Tamb., Tri.

Celtic Folksongs
Arranged by PAUL LAVENDER

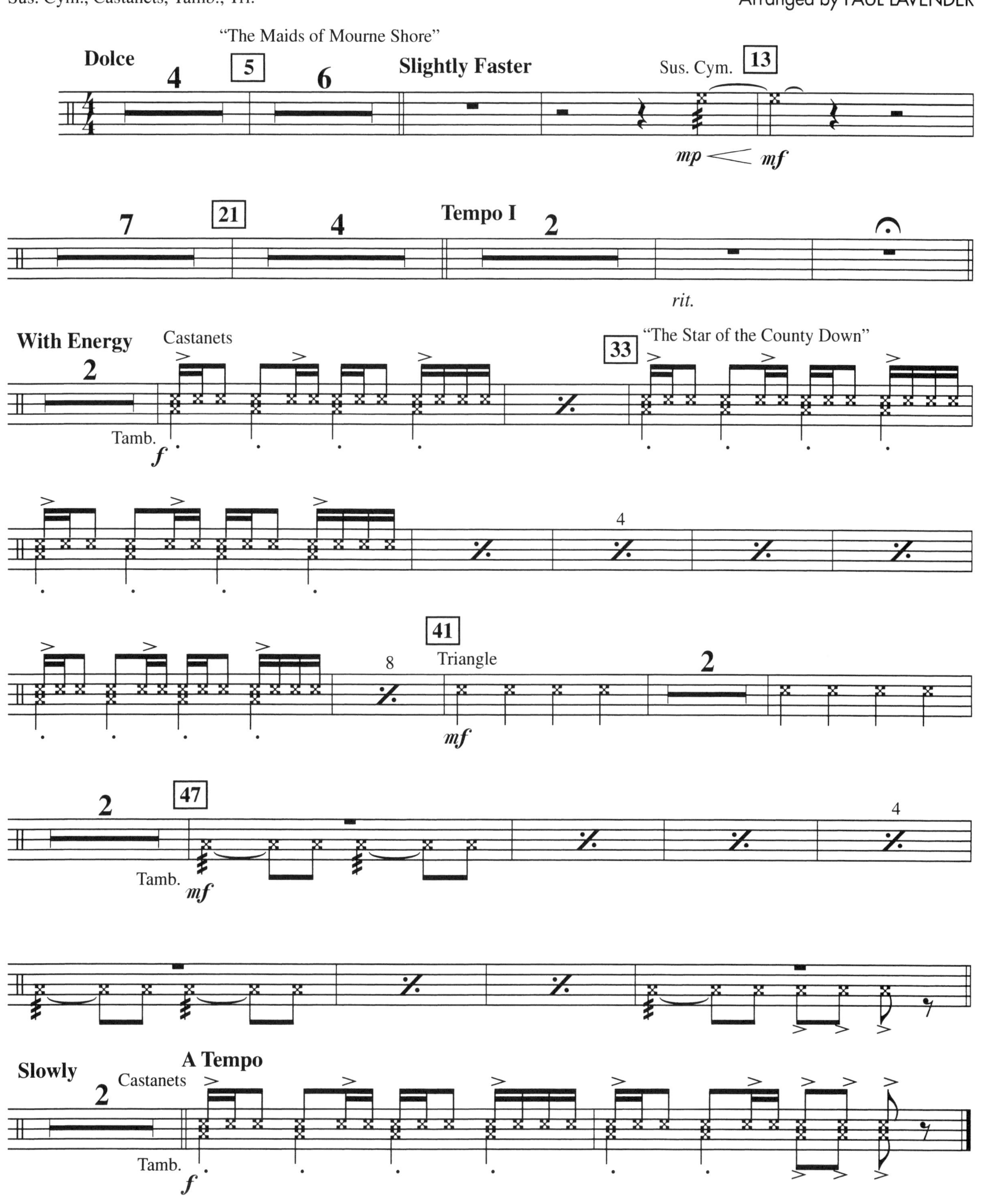